Carolina Hein

Laura Mulvey, Visual Pleasure and Narrative Cinen

Carolina Hein

Laura Mulvey, Visual Pleasure and Narrative Cinema

GRIN Verlag

Bibliografische Information der Deutschen Nationalbibliothek: Die Deutsche Bibliothek
verzeichnet diese Publikation in der Deutschen Nationalbibliografie; detaillierte bibliografische Daten sind im Internet über http://dnb.d-nb.de/ abrufbar.

1. Auflage 2006
Copyright © 2006 GRIN Verlag
http://www.grin.com/
Druck und Bindung: Books on Demand GmbH, Norderstedt Germany
ISBN 978-3-638-95275-0

Carolina Hein

Universität Konstanz

"Woman as image, man as bearer of the look"

Laura Mulvey, Visual Pleasure and Narrative Cinema

Table of contents

I.   The image of men and women in society

In a time of rapid technological progress and development, everything changes quite fast. These changes can be seen in every field of life. For instance, the way of supplying basic needs or the way how to make own life better, but also certain norms and values are quite different today. Instead of visiting a theatre in order to be entertained, people can watch TV or use the internet. If a man and a woman live together unmarried, hardly anybody will be shoked about that fact.

But often certain attitudes are anchored in society and can hardly be changed. One example is the detemination which individual role men and women are likely to play as members of a society and how their image appears in every culture. It is especially interesting to see how the media represent women, the so called ⸢weaker sex⸥

The following pages respond with the representation of women through the years. Additionally, they deal with problems and consequences coming up because of the difference between men and women.

II.   ⸢Woman as image, man as bearer of the look⸥, Laura Mulvey, *Visual Pleasure and Narrative Cinema*

1   Laura Mulvey criticises Hollywood film because of representing women as objects for the male gaze

The British feminist film-maker and theorist Laura Mulvey, born in 1941, wrote her essays, when Women's Liberation widely started to criticise discrimination of women. In *Visual and Other Pleasures*, published in 1975, Laura Mulvey investigates the content, the form of the film and the language of the film, combined in relation to the Gender. She looks into the subject of women represented by Hollywood cinema. In doing so, the author criticises the way female identity is formed by media. According to Laura Mulvey,

mainstream film satisfies especially the male spectator by projecting his desires on the screen. Women are regarded as objects of fetishistic display for male viewers' pleasure.

Fundamentally, a woman presented on the screen scene should be very erotic, so that she attracts the spectator`s attention. But a woman shown in films does not only appeal to the male spectators as a sexual object, furthermore, the female figure is regarded as a menace of castration, because a woman does not have a penis (21). To emphasise her opinion, Laura Mulvey alludes to Hollywood films shot between the nineteenthirties up to the nineteensixties.

Laura Mulvey associates male position with active and female position with passive (19). Due to the fact that women tend to exhibitionism, they are the object that men look at. The author transfers the terms of passive and active to the audience and the narrative cinema. The spectator embodies the subject, so to say the active role, while the narrative film stands for the object which is the passive position.

Beyond that, Laura Mulvey brings out in her essays mechanisms and codes of the Hollywood cinema which display heroes and heroines. In addition, she looks at its impact on spectators that serves both scopophilia, pleasure in looking at another person as an erotic object and narcissism by identification with the male protagonist (25).

2   Subordination of women because of male and female distinctions

Talking about Gender, first of all, it is important to mention that Gender does not stand for biological differences. Rather, this term corresponds to any social construction that has to do with the difference of men and women, such as personality and behaviour (British Literature and Culture 1, Semesterplan SS 2005-03-30, p. 138). Cultural ideologies and institutions annul the equality of men and women and stress that both are different (139). In particular, the difference becomes apparent when women make culture or represent culture.

One of the writers who targets the subordination of women is Sherry B. Ortner. The feminist historian and Professor of Anthropology was born in 1941. Her essay *Is Female to Male as Nature Is to Culture?* was published in 1974, almost parallel to Mulvey's *Visual and Other Pleasures.* Sherry B. Ortner refers to the subordination and devaluation of

women all over the world. According to her, oppression and devaluation result among other facts from ⌈cultural ideology⌉influenced by patriarchal order, by relating women to impurity, but also by prohibiting to be part, e.g. of certain ceremonies (493-494).

As an example for subordination she sets China. Despite the fact that the ideology of Taoism combines in its ⌈yin⌉and ⌈yan⌉both female and male elements in order to create balance and even, in spite of the fact that Kuan Yin is the central divinity and women's powerful and influential status, patriarchy still dominates China (492-493).

Moreover, Sherry B. Ortner finds out that the treatment of women, the degree of their influence and how much they do for the community, are different in every culture (492). In her opinion, there are three major problems of women's situations in all societies. Women have a global ⌈second-class status⌉, ⌈ideologies, symbolizations, and socio-structural arrangements⌉concerning women look diverse in different cultures and anything contributed by women is incompatible with ⌈cultural ideology⌉(493). It is neccessary to mention that a woman is simply a ⌈bearer⌉, not the creator of relevance like a man, because women live in patriarchy (Mulvey, 15).

Then, Sherry B. Ortner points out why men are oppressing women by emphasising that differences of men and women, above all strong and weak points developed by culture, establish the opinion that men are predominant, while women are inferior (495). From her point of view, each culture is preserving and protecting important forms such as ⌈symbols⌉ by methods that give the power to control nature. In rituals you can see, that culture has control over life and regulates everything that is happening in the world (496).

In every culture exists the thought that uncontrolled natural energies pollute anything that crosses its way. So, rituals of purity take a strong effect on the operation of natural energies. As culture wields power over nature, culture dominates. Because of ⌈their body and its functions⌉and their ⌈psychic structure⌉which are both closer to nature, social roles played by women are not that important than a man's cultural role (497). Therefore, women are related to nature, while men are related to culture (496-497). Since nature is inferior to culture, women are subordinated to men. The result is that women have to suffer from subordination and devaluation.

3 Women as male desire and fear

3.1 Female castration and women as castrators

In order to explain fetishism, Laura Mulvey quotes Sigmund Freud. In the opinion of
Freud, fetishism deflects from female castration by harmless objects which are ⸢signs⸣ for
the lack of a penis (10). Fetish objects such as cigarettes, whips or tight shoes with high
heels as Vivian wears it in the romantic comedy ⸢Pretty Woman⸣ create ⸢phallic
extension⸣ (8). Beyond that, women without a phallus are disciplined and punished by
fetish objects. The ⸢sign⸣ has a stimulating effect on the fantasy and corresponds to the
⸢sign of phallus⸣ (10). When men look at female genitals, men fear that they could lose
their own phallus. The dread of castration makes men concentrate on other objects instead
of women's genitals.

Women try to compensate their lack of a penis, but they can not escape from being a
treat of castration (14). Freud mentions the Medusa's head, although the Medusa herself is
not considered as a woman. For the reason that the Medusa's hair consist of snakes, the
Medusa symbolises the ⸢terror of castration⸣ (6). But snakes weaken the male fear,
because they look like the penis that the Medusa is missing and wherefore she appears to
be the horror of castration.

3.2 Women's image in male unconsciousness

Men playing the active role enjoy ⸢voyeurism⸣ Compared with men, women who are
given the passive role are the ones who reflect their feminin charme on show. Thus,
women have to bear the gaze of the spectator (7). Referring to ⸢Pretty Woman⸣ the
beautiful prostitute Vivian Ward exhibits her feminine charms in figure-hugging, short
clothes by striking a sexy pose at the bus stop. While walking, Vivian's hips move in a
provocative way. Hence, Vivian is drawing the male attention onto herself.

Laura Mulvey stresses that women are projections of male ⸢narcissistic fantasies⸣ (13).
In order to underline and to confirm this statement, Laura Mulvey names Allen Jones.
Allen Jones' series of sculptures at Tooth`s Gallery in London presented women with an
erotic impact, simultaneously looking like slaves (6). Serving as tables and chairs the

sculptures had an ⌈erected posture⌉as if they existed outside of time and space (12). In this way, Allen Jones indicates how the image of women appears to him, but also to ⌈the male unconscious⌉, namely as human beings who live without any deeper meaning or important functions and contributions (7).

4   Cinema

4.1   Functions and effects of the cinema

Through technology, cinema has changed over the years. New technics of the camera change the look and do not concentrate on a special look (25). Furthermore, the camera brings out certain important details. As the recording camera makes it hardly possible to see where the screen space ends, it gives the power to the (male) hero to rule the ⌈stage⌉(20).

There are three looks that are connected in the film (25). Firstly, the look of the ⌈camera⌉which records everything that happens in front of it. Secondly, that of the ⌈audience⌉that observes the events on the screen as soon as the film is ready to be performed. Finally, the look of the ⌈characters⌉who look at each other while performing within the fictive world. The narrative film is stressing especially on the view of characters, because they make the camera appear to be absent. Hence, the absence of the camera offers a world of illusion. If the audience does not perceive the recording camera, the spectators subconsciously experience what is going on on the screen. Even more, film characters can play their roles with ⌈verisimilitude⌉within the diegesis (26). According to Laura Mulvey, camera and audience, of course, are necessary in order to underline ⌈reality, obviousness and truth⌉to the narrative film (25).

Combining both the film that exercises power over ⌈time⌉and the film that controls ⌈space⌉, cinema brings via its cinematic codes ⌈illusion⌉to existence, because a new world combined with ⌈an object⌉and voyeurism developes (25). The dichotomic functions of the cinema consist furthermore in ⌈scopophilia⌉, that is, the spectator is sexually stimulated by looking at a female person, and identification with the main male protagonist (21).

Sitting in the film theatre, the audience is confronted with the difference between the darkness in the room hall and the light of the screen. In this manner, the spectator thinks that he is the only one who can gaze at the performers, because he takes part in events in his □private world□(17).

On closer inspection, Laura Mulvey points out that the fascination of Hollywood originates from the fact that Hollywood strategically changes □visual pleasure□by coding □the erotic into the language of the dominant patriarchal order□(16). This leads to the next topic.

4.2 Representation of women as image in the film

4.2.1 The male protagonist has power over the events and over the woman

To begin with, □as the bearer of the look of the spectator□the man has the power to change things within the film (20). The screen is his element, where the male protagonist controls the process in order to bring forward the action in the world of illusion. Compared with the film □Pretty Woman□ the successful and ruthless businessman Edward Lewis is in a powerful professional positiion. By buying companies in order to dismantling them for the purpose of selling the pieces for profit he exercises his power.

What is more, the film is only created around the main male character. The man's function in a film consists in evoking the spectator's identification with the male protagonist, so that the spectator comes into the main male character's position.

In addition, the performing man on the screen embodies □the more powerful ideal ego□ (20). According to the French psychoanalyst Jacques Lacan, the ideal ego developes, when a child sees his image in a mirror (17). Like the own image recognised in the mirror, the main male protagonist has even more power in influencing the story than the spectator has(20). In this case, Edward rules over many working places, because he can wind up enterprises. An example of his power is the scene when Edward makes unequivocally clear to the industrialist James Morse that he can not escape the fact that Edward will acquire the Morse Enterprises.

As the spectator identifies with the male protagonist, the spectator not only controls the world within the film but he also controls the woman. In ⌐Pretty Woman⌐Edward wants Vivian to buy conservative clothes like a dress in order to make her look like a Lady. Then, phoning Vivian from a private office Edward indirectly interdicts her to answer the phone.

Moreover, the spectator gets a ⌐sense of omnipotence⌐(20). This is the reason why the female performer belongs both to the main male character and indirectly to the audience that identifies itself with the man.

Analysing the film *To Have and Have Not* Laura Mulvey comes to the conclusion that as soon as the beautiful performing woman falls in love with the male protagonist, the man becomes the owner of her. Consequently, her attractiveness only applies to the man. And this is the case in ⌐Pretty Woman⌐ At the beginning of the film, the prostitute Vivian is very self-confident and intelligent. She has style and personality and knows how to perform female charme in order to find clients. Moreover, Vivian is acting informal and laughs vulgarly. But when Edward introduces her into the wealthy society in this particular week, when she keeps him company, Vivian has to pay attention to her mode of expression, her language and her behaviour. In the society of the upper class, she acts reserved. That is why she feels initially quite uncomfortable. In Edward's presence and that of the audience, but not of that of other characters, Vivian shows her ⌐glamorous characteristics⌐by her laughing and talking (21).

Being Edward's accompanion, Vivian wears elegant, not provocative clothes that do not accentuate her femininity. So, only the main male protagonist but also the spectator can avail oneselves from her beauty in different scenes.

4.2.2   Woman influences the man's feelings and his acts

In the film, the woman fulfils two tasks. On one hand, she is said to be the ⌐erotic object⌐ for the performers. On the other hand, a woman is also an ⌐erotic object⌐for everyone belonging to the audience (19). A performing woman as ⌐icon⌐is to be looked at (21).

Beyond that, a woman can always mean castration to the male spectator. Fetishistic scopophilia, however, turns the woman into an object of sexual stimulation. Therefore, the threat of castration disappears, while fetishism makes a woman become harmless (21). Voyeurism is also a possibility to avoid castration. In opposition to scopophilia, voyeurism satisfies while the male protagonist, but also the spectator tend to blame the woman. After the ⬜battle of will and strenght⬜has finished, the main male character forgives or punishes the woman (21-22).

Edward avoids castration, as he investigates Vivian by talking to her and going to the opera (Mulvey, 21). In this way, he gets to know the fascinating and also mysterious Vivian even better. Thus, Vivian loses her ⬜mystery⬜(21).

Laura Mulvey shows that women are important components of the film, although their sexual looks might interrupt the story (19). In this case, she quotes Budd Boetticher who was of the opinion that the female performer is only necessary, because the woman has an effect as well as on the male protagonist's emotions or actions (19). As soon as the film concentrates on woman's sexual appeal, the film leaves time and space (19-20). According to Mulvey, this happens when Marylin Monroe appears for the first time in *The River of No Return.*

Vivian's influence on Edward is quite strong. Vivian's warm and kindly nature changes Edward by bringing out his positive characteristics, e.g. sympathy and humanity. Consequently, Edward decides to help James Morse to rescue Morse Enterprises. At first, Vivian's declaration of love makes him feel confused. But Edward learns to allow his feelings and realises that he really loves Vivian.

III. Hollywood cinema still exploits the image of women

In the course of time, new fantastic objects have been invented in order to make life of people more comfortable. Connected with the still proceeding globalisation taking place all over the world, the international culture exchange has increased. But also the knowledge of different cultures has been broaden. Nowadays, people tolerate other cultures as well as its traditions.

Because of many important inventions, acquired knowledge, better hygienic conditions people regard their species as the most intelligent one. But no one can deny that despite great achievements of the twenty-first century, there are still problems that have to be eliminated. Obsolete ideas globally make life of women difficult. Even today, mass media present women from the male point of view. Hollywood cinema keeps on satisfying only the male desire. Thus, the following question arises: When will men regard women as equal persons to them and stop subordinating women?

Bibliography

Primary source

1. Mulvey, Laura, *Visual and Other Pleasures,* Palgrave Macmillan, 1989,
   p. 6 - 26

Secondary sources

2. *British Literature and Culture 1*, Semesterplan SS 2005-03-30, ⌐Gender⌐
   p. 138 -142; p. 491 ⌐497

3. ⌐Pretty Woman⌐ directed by Garry Marshall, Touchstone, 1990

CPSIA information can be obtained
at www.ICGtesting.com
Printed in the USA
LVIC040859300112

2671LVUK00001B